CW01082661

Original title:

Artful Living

Editor: Theodor Taimla

Author: Meelis Maurus

ISBN HARDBACK: 978-9916-87-058-7

ISBN PAPERBACK: 978-9916-87-059-4

Masterpieces of the Imagination

In shadows deep, ideas bloom,
Whispers dance in the quiet room.
A canvas filled with dreams untold,
Wonders crafted, bold and gold.

Each stroke of thought, a tale to weave,
Mysteries hidden for hearts to believe.
Through the lens of time, visions flare,
An artist's heart laid open, bare.

In realms where colors blend and flow,
Magic stirs in the afterglow.
Stories paint with every hue,
Inspirations born from skies so blue.

Until the light of day is past,
Imagination's spell holds fast.
From nothingness to vibrant scenes,
Creation breathes through drills and means.

So let us wander through the mind,
Where all the world's dreams are intertwined.
In masterpieces both grand and small,
The art of wonder shall enthrall.

Whispers of the Palette

Softly the colors murmur,
In whispers, they unite.
Each hue speaks a language,
Of passion and of light.

From crimson to gentle blue,
A symphony unfolds.
In the dance of the colors,
A story yet untold.

The palette holds the secrets,
Of every vibrant shade.
With every drop of paint,
A memory is made.

Brushes sway like dancers,
On this canvas of dreams.
Creating silent magic,
In vibrant, flowing streams.

In the stillness of creation,
We find our hearts' release.
With whispers of the palette,
Comes a moment of peace.

Dance of the Colorful Heart

In the rhythm of life,
Colors pulse and play.
The heart beats in patterns,
In a bright ballet.

Brushes twirl like dancers,
Spinning wild and free.
Each stroke tells a story,
Of who we're meant to be.

With laughter in each stroke,
And tears that blend with grace,
The canvas captures moments,
In this wild, vibrant space.

Emotions swirl like colors,
In a radiant embrace.
The dance of the heart sings,
In every brush's trace.

In this vibrant symphony,
Our spirits find their part.
A dance that celebrates,
The beauty of the heart.

Brushstrokes of Existence

Life is painted freely,
In tones both bright and dark.
With each brushstroke taken,
We leave behind a mark.

Moments captured in colors,
Like sunlight through the trees,
Each hue a reminder,
Of life's flowing breeze.

Brushstrokes of existence,
Tell tales of joy and pain.
In the palette of our days,
Both struggle and refrain.

With every fading sunset,
And each dawn's first light,
We forge our everlasting,
In the canvas of our sight.

So let the colors mingle,
And dreams begin to flow.
In the brushstrokes of existence,
We paint the life we know.

Serenity in Strokes

Brush to canvas, calm descends,
Nature's beauty, as silence bends.
Each gentle stroke, a breath of peace,
In colors rich, let worries cease.

Tranquil shades of blue unwind,
Heartbeats sync with the gentle kind.
The world fades in hues of white,
Serenity found in this soft light.

Moments captured, still and bright,
A tranquil scene in morning light.
Whispers of green, a sigh so clear,
In strokes of calm, the soul draws near.

As the seasons gracefully change,
The palette shifts, yet feels so strange.
Nature's embrace, a soothing balm,
In each creation, the heart feels calm.

So let the art be your retreat,
In every stroke, find life's heartbeat.
Serenity wrapped in colors pure,
In the sanctuary of art, find cure.

Canvas of Dreams

In the silence of night,
Stars weave tales untold.
Each brushstroke a wish,
A longing to unfold.

Colors blend in harmony,
As thoughts begin to soar.
A canvas filled with hopes,
An open, endless door.

Visions dance like shadows,
In the moon's gentle light.
Each hue a reflection,
Of dreams burning bright.

With every stroke, a journey,
Into the vast unknown.
A tapestry of wonders,
In the heart's sacred zone.

As twilight softly lingers,
The world finds its embrace.
In the canvas of the soul,
We find our hidden space.

Colors of the Heartbeat

In every pulse, a shade appears,
A tapestry woven from joy and tears.
Crimson reds for the love we share,
Blues of sadness, a heart laid bare.

Golden yellows light the day,
Shades of joy that come to play.
Greens of growth, of life anew,
In every color, emotions true.

Violet dreams that weave the night,
Sparks of inspiration take their flight.
Each color tells a story bright,
In the palette of our heart's delight.

As the canvas fills, we take our stand,
Echoes of pulse drawn by gentle hand.
A masterpiece crafted from every beat,
In hues of life, our hearts repeat.

So let the colors sing their tune,
In the sunlight, and under the moon.
Each heartbeat brings a vibrant spark,
Unfolding stories in the dark.

Crafting Life's Narrative

Words collide like stars at night,
Tales of love, of loss, of light.
Each sentence, crafted with intent,
A journey through where moments went.

In whispers soft, the stories flow,
Time-stamped memories, ebb and glow.
Through laughter shared and silence steeped,
A narrative born, its essence reaped.

Pages turn as seasons pass,
Reflections trapped in transparent glass.
The ink bleeds truth, the heartbeats rhyme,
Life unfolds within the line.

So pen your dreams and carve your way,
In every phrase, let spirit sway.
A tapestry woven in ink and heart,
Crafting life's narrative, a sacred art.

In the end, as the story holds,
Through valleys deep and hills of gold,
We find our place, our voice, our part,
In crafting life, we weave the heart.

A Dance of Shadows

In the twilight's gentle sway,
Whispers flicker, dance and play,
Shadows twist beneath the moon,
In silence, they find their tune.

Echoes shimmer, soft and bright,
Forming shapes in the night,
A ballet of dark and light,
In dreams they take to flight.

Veils of dusk, they softly weave,
Tales of hearts that dare to grieve,
Find the solace in the dark,
Where each shadow leaves a mark.

Time stands still in this embrace,
Every movement finds its place,
Crafted moments, swift as air,
A dance of shadows, light as care.

The Muse Within

Deep in the quiet place of thought,
Where dreams are spun and battles fought,
A whisper tugs with gentle gleam,
The muse awakens, starts to dream.

Colors burst from silent hues,
Words collide and form new views,
Inspiration flows like streams,
From the heart it gently beams.

In shadowed corners, ideas bloom,
Bringing light to every room,
Each stroke a brush of fate,
Creating worlds, it can't wait.

The canvas waits, an open heart,
For every dream to play its part,
The muse within, forever bright,
Guides the hand into the night.

Journals of the Imagination

Pages filled with whispered thoughts,
Captured dreams, the mind's own knots,
Letters dance, and stories sway,
In journals where the muses play.

Ink flows like a river wide,
Carving paths where visions glide,
Each entry holds a piece of soul,
Captured moments that make us whole.

Time bends in the written line,
Fleeting thoughts in inked design,
Adventures penned with every breath,
In the stillness, life and death.

A world unfolds in each small scribble,
Imagination's gentle dribble,
These journals keep the spirit free,
Guarding tales for all to see.

Crafting Moments

In the quiet of the dawn,
Where the world feels fresh and drawn,
We gather fragments, sharp and clear,
Crafting moments, held so dear.

With every laugh that fills the air,
And every sigh, we lay it bare,
Each heartbeat in this fleeting time,
A tapestry spun, a rhythmic rhyme.

We weave our days like threads of gold,
In memory's embrace, legends told,
Moments stitched with care and grace,
In the fabric of our space.

Every glance, each soft embrace,
Brings life to time in this small place,
Crafting moments, rich and bright,
In the shadows and the light.

Threads of Inspired Thought

In the quiet of night,
Ideas begin to bloom.
Whispers of dreams take flight,
Illuminating the room.

Each thread woven tight,
A tapestry of grace.
Capturing the light,
In this sacred space.

Moments like a spark,
Igniting the unknown.
Guiding through the dark,
To the heart's soft tone.

Wisdom softly flows,
Like water in a stream.
In each thought that grows,
We find our way, our dream.

Embrace the unknown,
Let curiosity guide.
With every seed sown,
Inspired hearts collide.

A Dance with Chaos

In the whirlwind's spin,
I lose and find my way.
The mirror shows the din,
Where shadows dance and play.

In the clash and roar,
Harmony takes its stand.
Disorder at my door,
Yet peace holds out a hand.

Steps weave in and out,
A rhythm of the wild.
In chaos, there's a shout,
Of freedom unbeguiled.

Fleeting moments flow,
Like leaves upon the stream.
In chaos, there's a glow,
A surreal, vivid dream.

So let the music rise,
Embrace the flowing tide.
In chaos, hear the cries,
Of passion, wild and wide.

The Brush's Embrace

With gentle strokes it glides,
Across the canvas bare.
Colors in whispers bide,
A dance beyond compare.

Each hue a secret told,
In shades both bright and deep.
Stories yet unfold,
In dreams we dare to keep.

A splash of hope appears,
As shadows fade away.
Through laughter and through tears,
The brush begins to play.

In every line, a heart,
In every shade, a soul.
Creating from the start,
The artist feels it whole.

Artistry takes flight,
In every vivid line.
In this soft, pure light,
The brush and heart entwine.

Reflections in a Prism

Through the glass, I see,
A world of split delight.
Colors dance like glee,
In shimmering, pure light.

Each facet tells a tale,
Of dreams that intertwine.
In reflections, we sail,
On hope's serene design.

Moments caught in time,
Fragments of what has been.
In rhythm, they chime,
As past and future blend.

With every ray that bends,
The spectrum will unfold.
A journey never ends,
In shades both fierce and bold.

So gaze into the glass,
Let wonder be your guide.
In reflections, let pass,
The beauty held inside.

Colors of the Morning

The sun yawns in golden light,
Breaking shadows, taking flight.
Whispers of a new day born,
Painting skies in hues, adorn.

Birds sing soft in joyful tune,
As light dances with the moon.
Morning glories stretch and rise,
Embracing warmth from sapphire skies.

Breezes carry scents so sweet,
Fresh beginnings greet our feet.
Dewdrops shimmer, diamonds bright,
Morning's palette, pure delight.

Clouds drift gently, white like dreams,
Reflecting all of nature's schemes.
Each color tells a tale untold,
In the dawn, life's beauty unfolds.

A canvas wide, forever new,
With strokes of pink, and vibrant blue.
In every shade, a promise glows,
The colors of the morning flows.

Celestial Canvases

Stars shimmer bright,
Painting the night.
Galaxies swirl,
A cosmic whirl.

Colors collide,
In silence they bide.
Nebulas bloom,
In endless room.

Planets align,
In harmony they shine.
Moonlight whispers,
Dreams it stirs.

Comets race by,
Across the sky.
Wonders unveil,
On an astral trail.

Eclipses reveal,
Mysteries to feel.
In this vast sea,
We dare to be.

The Art of Pause

In a world that rushes by,
Moments pause to let us sigh.
Embrace the stillness, take a breath,
In silence lies a subtle depth.

Nature whispers, time stands still,
A gentle urge, a quiet thrill.
Breathe in peace, release your cares,
In the now, find solace rare.

A cup of tea, warm in hand,
Glimmers of time softly planned.
Let thoughts drift like autumn leaves,
In the pause, our spirit weaves.

Close your eyes, listen within,
Feel the calm where dreams begin.
Connection blooms beneath the sky,
In the pause, we learn to fly.

With every heartbeat, joy will rise,
Awakening to life's surprise.
Celebrate the art of rest,
In the stillness, we are blessed.

Spirit in Every Stroke

With brush in hand, the canvas waits,
A world of colors, love creates.
Every stroke, a heartbeat's dance,
Inviting dreams, a second chance.

Whirls of life on fabric spin,
Echoes of the heart within.
Each layer tells a story deep,
Awakening the soul from sleep.

Splashes bright, emotions burst,
From quiet whispers, art's the first.
Hands of passion paint the view,
In every hue, a spirit true.

The muse inspires, visions flow,
An artist's heart begins to grow.
In every line, a feeling found,
With every stroke, the peace is crowned.

Unfolding beauty, brush by brush,
In vibrant silence, create the hush.
Art connects the spirit's core,
With every stroke, we open doors.

Dance of the Everyday

Morning breaks in gold,
As stories unfold.
Feet tap to the beat,
Life's rhythm so sweet.

Chores turn to grace,
Each moment a space.
The laughter, the sighs,
In mundane disguise.

Nature joins the show,
With winds that softly blow.
Leaves twirl around,
On the ground they're found.

Children at play,
Chasing dreams and rays.
The world spins along,
In its vibrant song.

Night wraps in calm,
With stars like a balm.
Dreams waltz through the air,
In our hearts we share.

Tints of Togetherness

In the tapestry of life we weave,
Colors blend, hearts believe.
Side by side, our stories join,
Tints of togetherness, we coin.

Hand in hand through joy and strife,
Painting moments, the hues of life.
Laughter mingles, smiles unite,
In every shade, our love ignites.

Sharing dreams beneath the sun,
Embracing all, we are as one.
Every color, every tone,
Whispers of a love we've grown.

Through storms and calm, we hug the light,
In darkest hours, our bond ignites.
Together, we create the art,
With every tint, we heal the heart.

In unity, we find our song,
A melody where we belong.
With every stroke, a bond so true,
Tints of togetherness, me and you.

Lines of Thought

Thoughts intertwined,
Life's pathways defined.
Whispers of truth,
In the mind's booth.

In moments we pause,
To shake off our flaws.
Words formed in light,
Shine through the night.

Questions arise,
Seeking the skies.
Time flows like sand,
In the heart's hand.

Fragments of dreams,
Flow like new streams.
Building a bridge,
Life's gentle ridge.

Clarity found,
In silence profound.
Lines come alive,
In thoughts we thrive.

Tapestry of Dreams

In shadows deep, we weave our thread,
A tapestry where hopes are spread.
With whispers soft, the night unfolds,
As dreams take flight, in starlit scolds.

Each color bright, a story told,
Of laughter shared and hearts of gold.
In gentle hues, our visions dance,
A vivid world, born of romance.

The moonlight glimmers on our skin,
As melodies begin within.
With every stitch, our lives we sew,
A journey where the wild winds blow.

With every heartbeat, threads entwine,
A fabric rich, divine design.
In dreams we trust, we find our way,
Through night and day, forever stay.

United we, through thick and thin,
A tapestry where love can win.
Our stories woven, strong and bright,
In every shade, we find our light.

A Palette of Possibilities

With strokes of gold and splashed deep blue,
The canvas waits, for me and you.
Creation whispers, soft and clear,
A palette bright, our dreams appear.

Each brush a chance, each hue a side,
In vibrant tones, our spirits glide.
With every mix, a world takes form,
In colors bold, we break the norm.

The reds of passion, greens of earth,
In every shade, we find our worth.
A swirling dance of light and shade,
In this vast world, our hopes cascade.

From pastels soft to fiery blaze,
Our visions swirl in painted haze.
The beauty blooms in every line,
A masterpiece, our hearts entwine.

Embrace the stroke, let colors sing,
In every shade, new life will spring.
With every dream, we chase the sky,
In our own world, we'll surely fly.

The Essence of Beauty

In whispered sighs, the gentle breeze,
We find the beauty that can please.
With every petal, soft and bright,
The essence glows, a pure delight.

A fleeting glance, a tender smile,
In every moment, pause a while.
The sun will rise, the moon will fall,
In nature's grace, we find it all.

From mountains high to oceans deep,
The beauty wakes from silent sleep.
In every shadow, light will play,
A dance of life, both night and day.

In every laugh, in every tear,
The essence blooms, so crystal clear.
A tapestry of joy extends,
In beauty found, our spirit bends.

So cherish moments, big and small,
The essence of beauty, binds us all.
In every heart, a song will start,
In every breath, the soul will art.

Chasing Light

Across the fields, we run and roam,
In pursuit of light, we find our home.
The dawn awakens, soft as dreams,
In golden rays, our spirit gleams.

With every step, we feel the chase,
The light embracing, our warm grace.
With open hearts, we seek to soar,
In endless skies, forevermore.

The shadows fade, the night retreats,
As we follow where the light beats.
In every sunrise, hope is drawn,
A brand new day, the darkness gone.

As twilight paints, the stars ignite,
We hold the moments, pure and bright.
The chase continues, never ends,
In chasing light, our soul ascends.

So let us run, with hearts ablaze,
In every dawn, our spirit plays.
Chasing the light, hand in hand,
Together we, like grains of sand.

Whisps of Creativity

Ideas take flight,
In the soft twilight.
Brush strokes of thought,
In each moment caught.

Words sway and dance,
In a timeless trance.
Imagination flows,
Where the wild wind goes.

Colors merge and collide,
Art's daring ride.
Voices softly hum,
In a world yet to come.

Echoes of dreams,
Burst at the seams.
Capture and mold,
In stories retold.

Crafting the unknown,
In fields we have sown.
Whispers of the soul,
Making us whole.

Mosaics of Everyday Moments

A cup of tea on a rainy day,
Sunlight dances through the gray,
Children laugh, games unfold,
Memories whispered, stories told.

Fingers trace on weathered wood,
In quiet corners, peace feels good,
Footsteps linger on sandy shores,
Life's small wonders, that's what it stores.

Puddles shimmer, reflections play,
A gentle breeze, it sweeps away,
Old books stacked in a cozy nook,
Lost in tales, one's spirit took.

Morning light through window pane,
Birdsong echoes, a soft refrain,
Moments fleeting, yet they shine,
In the mundane, a spark divine.

Dinner shared with laughter loud,
Underneath the evening cloud,
Hands entwined, a simple touch,
In these moments, we find so much.

Symphony of Strokes

Brushes dance on canvas wide,
Colors blend, emotions glide,
Whispers of the painter's heart,
Each stroke a brand, a work of art.

A canvas bare calls for the light,
Shadows deepen, day turns night,
Figures leap from shades unknown,
Life emerges, in paint it's shown.

The symphony of hues so bright,
In every layer, depth and light,
From chaos born, a vision forms,
An artist battles, beauty storms.

Palette rich with dreams untold,
Secrets hidden, visions bold,
Creation breathes with every line,
A journey through the hands divine.

In quiet moments, inspiration flows,
With passion's fire, the spirit grows,
Each painting tells a tale anew,
A symphony from heart to view.

Echoes of Inspired Souls

Voices whisper in the night,
Stories shared, hearts take flight,
Through the veil, a dream is spun,
Echoes linger, shadows run.

The canvas blank, the notes unheard,
Inspiration waits, in silence stirred,
A spark ignites, the spirit sings,
In every heart, creation springs.

In midnight oil, ideas glow,
Underneath the moon's soft show,
Words become a gentle tide,
With every yearning, dreams abide.

Together we weave, a tapestry bright,
Of hopes and fears, love's pure light,
In the echoes, we find our place,
Inspired souls in time and space.

Every heartbeat, every sigh,
Carries whispers to the sky,
Through the ages, we impart,
Echoes fade, yet not the art.

Tapestry of the Mundane

Coffee brews in morning haze,
Daily rituals, life's soft praise,
The rhythm of a day begun,
In small details, joy is spun.

Streets alive with voices near,
Familiar faces, smiles sincere,
In every glance, a story told,
In the mundane, warmth unfolds.

Evening falls, the world slows down,
Starlit whispers where dreams are found,
A favorite book, a quiet chair,
Within these moments, love laid bare.

Baking bread, the aroma sweet,
Gathered hopes in every beat,
Family laughter fills the air,
In these threads, life is laid bare.

The tapestry woven with hands so kind,
In the simple things, we find,
Life's true essence, a gentle refrain,
In the mundane, we grow and gain.

Between Light and Shadow

In the hush of dusk's embrace,
Whispers dance, the shadows trace.
Flickering dreams begin to bloom,
As hope weaves light within the gloom.

Stars collide in twilight's fold,
Stories whispered, secrets told.
Boundaries blur where night holds sway,
In the balance, night meets day.

A soft sigh in the silent air,
Fading edges, without a care.
In the pause where wishes fade,
Fleeting moments, memories made.

Crimson hues blend with the gray,
Breath of life in disarray.
Echoes linger, the past survives,
In stillness, the heart's peace thrives.

Between the realms, we find our way,
Caught in the dance of light's play.
With every step, we learn and grow,
In the twilight's gentle glow.

Sketches of a Vibrant Journey

Brush strokes color the canvas wide,
Every journey, a changing tide.
Sketched in hues of joy and pain,
A tapestry where dreams remain.

Footprints scatter across the land,
Each step taken, a guiding hand.
From the valleys to peaks so high,
Every heartbeat sings a lullaby.

Moments captured in fleeting light,
A vivid story takes its flight.
Through laughter shared and tears bestowed,
Every chapter, a winding road.

In the market of bustling streets,
The rhythm of life, a dance that beats.
Voices merge, creating a song,
In this vibrant world, we all belong.

With colors blending, tales unfold,
In every face, a story told.
The journey rich, the spirit free,
A vivid sketch of you and me.

The Elegance of Everyday

In morning's light, the world awakes,
The simple grace that kindness makes.
A quiet smile, a helping hand,
In daily moments, love will stand.

Coffee brews, the aroma spreads,
Familiar comfort in routines bred.
Each mundane task becomes a dance,
In the rhythm of life, we find our chance.

Conversations over shared meals,
Crafting memories that time reveals.
Between laughter and gentle sighs,
In these moments, the heart complies.

A walk through streets where life unfolds,
Stories carried, the young and old.
In every breath, a chance to see,
The elegance in you and me.

Under the stars, we come alive,
Together creating, we will thrive.
In the ordinary, beauty resides,
In the elegance of daily strides.

Visionaries in Motion

Eyes alight with dreams untold,
In every vision, futures hold.
Hearts beat strong with passion's fire,
Chasing dreams that lift us higher.

With each step, the world takes shape,
Inventing paths, we all escape.
Every challenge met with grace,
In the dance of time and space.

Ideas spark like flames at night,
Guiding us towards the light.
With every leap, a chance to soar,
Visionaries dreaming, wanting more.

In whispers shared and hopes ignited,
Passions merge, and goals united.
Through storms we sail, unbowed we stand,
Creating futures, hand in hand.

In motion, we redefine the skies,
With courage bold and daring eyes.
A journey bright where spirits meet,
As visionaries make life sweet.

Palette of Possibilities

Colors blend with gentle grace,
Dreams emerge in every space.
Brushes dance on canvas bright,
Painting visions, pure delight.

Whispers of the untried hue,
Each stroke brings something new.
Life's a canvas, vast and wide,
With every shade, let hope abide.

Textures weave a vibrant tale,
Inspiration sets the sail.
From shadows, brilliance will arise,
Creating worlds beneath the skies.

In the stillness, ideas bloom,
Infinite paths break through the gloom.
Let your heart be the guiding star,
On this journey, near or far.

Embrace the mess, the twist and turn,
In each failure, lessons earn.
With every layer, find your voice,
In this art, you have the choice.

Crafting Joy in Silence

In quiet corners, joy will thrive,
Whispers of the heart come alive.
Moments cherished, time stands still,
Crafting warmth with simple will.

Listen close to nature's song,
Where silence plays, we all belong.
Between the thoughts, a space to find,
The gentle peace of a tranquil mind.

Hands create with soft embrace,
In solitude, we find our grace.
Each heartbeat echoes pure and true,
A symphony composed for you.

In stillness, dreams are softly spun,
Woven threads of joy begun.
From quietude, connections bloom,
Filling hearts, dispelling gloom.

So cherish silence, hold it dear,
In every pause, the world will clear.
Crafting joy, both deep and wide,
In the stillness, we abide.

The Art of Being Present

Moments linger, gently sway,
In the now is where we play.
Time unfolds like petals soft,
In stillness, spirits lift aloft.

Awareness wraps each breath we take,
In simple joys, our souls awake.
Fragments of a fleeting day,
In presence, find our way.

Nature whispers in soft tones,
In every leaf, a heart in stones.
Grounded here, we cease to chase,
Finding beauty in this space.

Every glance, a story told,
In the present, we are bold.
Feel the pulse of life go by,
In every moment, let us fly.

So let us cherish what we see,
In this now, we are truly free.
The art of life, a dance divine,
In the present, hearts entwine.

Sculpted Moments in Time

Chiseling memories from the stone,
Each moment crafted, never alone.
Time's sculptor shapes with loving hands,
Creating beauty in life's strands.

Fleeting seconds, caught in grace,
Every smile, a warm embrace.
From shadows dark to brightened days,
Life's a gallery of endless ways.

With every breath, we carve our way,
In joy and sorrow, shades of gray.
In these moments, giants grow,
Sculpted truths begin to show.

Hands that mold, hearts that feel,
In the process, we reveal.
Eternity held in fleeting scenes,
Life's a tapestry of dreams.

So let us etch our stories fine,
In the sculpture of our time.
These moments cherished, never fade,
In the arts of life, we've made.

Mosaic of Memories

Fragments of laughter, pieces of dreams,
Colors that mingle, flowing like streams.
Time weaves a tapestry, rich and bright,
Every thread tells a tale, morning to night.

Dancing through shadows, whispers alive,
Echoes of moments, where spirits thrive.
A gentle reminder in each faded hue,
The stories of old blend with the new.

Photographs scattered, like leaves in the breeze,
Holding the essence of hearts at ease.
Moments entwined in a delicate dance,
Captured in time, lost in a trance.

Memories linger, like stars in the dark,
Flickering gently, igniting a spark.
In the quiet corners, they softly reside,
Guardians of history, our hearts' trusted guide.

A puzzle of laughter, a compilation of tears,
Treasures assembled throughout the years.
A mosaic of life, both fragile and grand,
Crafted with love, by fate's gentle hand.

Vibrations of the Visions

In the stillness, visions take flight,
Whispers of color in the dim light.
Echoes of dreams in the air we share,
Resounding softly, a musical flair.

Rippling waves of emotion arise,
Shifting and changing, like clouds in the skies.
Every heartbeat dances, rhythms collide,
In the music of life, we all coincide.

Vibrations surround us, alive with grace,
Each moment echoed in a timeless space.
From whispers of hope to shouts of delight,
The spectrum of feelings shines ever bright.

In silence, we listen to the world speak,
In every heartbeat, the strong and the weak.
A canvas of visions painted anew,
Colors merging in a beautiful hue.

Through shadows and light, we glide and sway,
Embracing the moments, come what may.
Each note a reminder that we are alive,
In the vibrations, together we thrive.

The Geometry of Feelings

Angles and curves in the heart's design,
Intersecting paths where souls intertwine.
Measured in laughter, or sometimes in tears,
The geometry of love transcends all fears.

Symmetry dances in the ebb and flow,
A balance of moments, the high and the low.
Triangles form in the warmth of a hug,
A circle of trust, snug as a bug.

Lines drawn in sand, ephemeral and sweet,
Yet intricate patterns under our feet.
In geometry's realm, our hearts can roam,
Finding each other, we build our home.

Parallel stories scripted in time,
Each vivid chapter, a rhythm, a rhyme.
With shapes resonating, emotions unite,
Creating a structure, both fragile and bright.

The angles remind us of paths we have crossed,
In the map of our feelings, no moment is lost.
For love is the compass that guides us along,
In this geometric dance, we are ever strong.

Capturing the Fleeting

Moments that flitter like leaves in the breeze,
Gone in a heartbeat, yet timeless, they freeze.
Captured in whispers, a glance, a sigh,
Fleeting, yet lasting, as clouds drift by.

Snapshots of sunlight, warm on our skin,
Fleeting impressions, where love can begin.
A sparkle of laughter, a gentle embrace,
Time's fleeting treasures, we yearn to trace.

In a blink, the world shifts, changes its hue,
Yet memories linger, both precious and true.
Like fleeting shadows dancing on walls,
We chase after echoes as silence falls.

Holding the transient, we weave every thread,
In the tapestry of life, where dreams are led.
Though moments may vanish like mist in the morn,
The essence remains, in our hearts reborn.

So let's cherish the fleeting, the briefest of light,
For in those swift seconds, our spirits take flight.
Capture the laughter, each sigh, every tear,
In the dance of the moment, we hold what is dear.

Brushstrokes of Freedom

In fields of gold, the sunlight gleams,
Brushstrokes dance, painting vivid dreams.
Wings unfold in a boundless sky,
Whispers of hope on a gentle sigh.

Through valleys deep, where shadows play,
Freedom calls, lighting the way.
Colors blend in a vibrant stream,
Every heartbeat, a shared dream.

With every brush, a story told,
A tapestry woven with threads of gold.
Nature hums in sweet refrain,
Embracing joy, releasing pain.

Under the stars, we find our place,
In the dance of night, we trace the grace.
Each moment fleeting, yet held so tight,
Brushstrokes of freedom in the night.

Guided by light, we follow our fate,
Brushing the canvas, we'll never wait.
For in each stroke, a promise lies,
To paint our truth beneath the skies.

The Texture of Existence

Life's a tapestry, woven fine,
Threads of joy and sorrow entwine.
Each moment a stitch in the vast expanse,
A rhythm of fate, a woven dance.

Seasons shift like a painter's hand,
Creating landscapes, vast and grand.
Fingers trace the lines of the past,
In the texture of life, our shadows cast.

Whispers of time, like grains of sand,
Shift and scatter, yet always stand.
Every heartbeat pulses with grace,
A reminder of truth in this sacred space.

Embracing colors, we cherish the mix,
In vibrant layers, our spirit picks.
The texture unfolds, revealing surprise,
In the quiet moments, our spirit flies.

In this existence, we find our way,
As we write our stories day by day.
The fabric of life, rich and raw,
A symphony of existence, we draw.

A Dance of Colors

On canvas bright, colors collide,
In joyful hues, our dreams reside.
Each brushstroke sings a sweet refrain,
A dance of colors, free from pain.

With every twist, the rhythms flow,
In laughter's light, our spirits glow.
Life's a carousel, spinning round,
In vibrant bursts, we're glory-bound.

We twirl on clouds, we leap on air,
In the dance of colors, we share.
The palette spills in joyous cheer,
In every shade, the world feels near.

Through storms and sun, the colors blend,
A harmony where dreams transcend.
In a whirl of light, we find our muse,
In a dance of colors, we choose.

So let us spin, let laughter play,
In the bright hues of a brand new day.
For in this dance, we break the mold,
A story of colors, waiting to be told.

Whispers of Time

In the still of night, whispers rise,
Echoing softly, under the skies.
Moments unfold like a fragile bloom,
Breathing stories, dispelling gloom.

The clock ticks gently, a lullaby,
Carrying dreams that float and fly.
Each second a pearl in the ocean vast,
Whispers of time, holding the past.

Shadows dance on the walls of our mind,
In the echoes of laughter, we find.
Glimmers of hope in a fleeting glance,
In the whispers of time, we take a chance.

Through corridors of memory we roam,
Finding our way, creating a home.
With every breath, a new tale begins,
In the whispers of time, love always wins.

So let's gather moments, hold them near,
For in whispers of time, nothing to fear.
In the heart of existence, our spirits climb,
Embracing the lessons in whispers of time.

The Color of Emotion

Whispers of blue paint the skies,
A gentle touch where the heart lies.
Passion ignites in a fiery red,
While quiet thoughts wear a cloak of dread.

Joy dances bright in vivid gold,
A smile that warms when the world feels cold.
Greens of envy creep through the day,
Shades of sadness, they drift away.

Every hue tells a tale so rare,
In the canvas of life, emotions flare.
Bold strokes of laughter, soft tears we shed,
With each splash, our secrets are spread.

Colors blend in a beautiful mess,
In chaos and calm, we find our rest.
The palette of feelings we can't ignore,
In artful existence, there's always more.

So paint your life in colors bright,
Let each emotion reveal your light.
For in the spectrum of all we share,
Love's vibrant brush strokes linger in air.

Life as a Masterpiece

Every moment, a stroke divine,
In the gallery of time, we align.
Brushes guided by dreams untold,
Crafting a story in colors bold.

With laughter's echo, the canvas fills,
Each heartbeat a rhythm, the spirit thrills.
Mistakes become shadows that deepen the line,
Each imperfection, a design so fine.

Through vibrant hues, we find our way,
In the art of living, we choose to stay.
With passion and purpose, our vision clear,
Life's masterpiece unfolds year by year.

In gentle strokes or wildest flair,
Art is the mirror of love and care.
Together we weave in intricate threads,
Creating a life where beauty spreads.

So cherish each color, let them embrace,
In every heartbeat, find your place.
For life is a canvas, rich and vast,
A masterpiece painted, a vision to last.

Sketches of Serenity

In tranquil strokes, the sun does rise,
Soft whispers blend in the morning skies.
A gentle breeze through the willow's sway,
Nature's embrace at the start of day.

The brush of silence, a calming guide,
In stillness, where our worries subside.
Pebbles ripple in a crystal stream,
Reflecting hopes that awaken dream.

Petals flutter in the softest light,
A tranquil canvas, the heart takes flight.
Serene moments weave through time's embrace,
As we sketch our dreams in this sacred space.

Mountains stand tall, cloaked in mist,
In quietude, life's chaos is kissed.
With every breath, the world we create,
In sketches of peace, we contemplate.

So let the colors of calm align,
In every heartbeat, find the divine.
For within the silence, our souls shall see,
The beauty of life, forever free.

Harmonies in Hues

Notes of color dance in the air,
A symphony rich, bold, and rare.
Brushes play like a sweet refrain,
In harmonies crafted from joy and pain.

Cadences of laughter, shades of delight,
Every hue sings through day and night.
Golden tones shimmer like a bright star,
As dreams unite in melodies afar.

The rhythm of life flows soft and sweet,
In every heartbeat, the colors meet.
Blues and greens waltz under the moon,
Creating a world where hearts are attuned.

With each stroke, a love song grows,
As vibrant stories of life compose.
Let the palette echo with every sound,
In harmonies of color, we're forever bound.

So dance in the spectrum, let spirits soar,
For in every hue, there's so much more.
In life's grand orchestra, we find our part,
Harmonies in hues, the language of the heart.

The Heart's Easel

Upon the canvas, colors blend,
Soft strokes of joy, where sorrows mend.
With every hue, a feeling drawn,
Life's palette blooms with each new dawn.

Brush against the quiet mind,
In gentle peace, the soul we find.
Each heartbeat shapes the art we wear,
Unfolding dreams with tender care.

Lines of laughter, shadows cast,
Echoes of a love that lasts.
Every blemish, every tear,
Adds to the beauty we hold dear.

In vibrant shades, our essence glows,
Nature's whispers, the heart knows.
The easel sways with every breath,
Creating warmth, defying death.

So let the colors freely dance,
A masterpiece of fate and chance.
Through trials faced, and triumphs won,
The heart's easel shines like the sun.

Shadows of Serenity

In twilight's hush, the shadows play,
Whispers soft, they gently sway.
Beneath the trees, where silence breathes,
The heart finds peace among the leaves.

Moonlight drapes a silver gown,
Cradling dreams in hopes not drown.
Amidst the stillness, thoughts take flight,
Guided by the stars' soft light.

Waves of calm in the evening air,
Filling hearts with tender care.
Each shadow tells a story bright,
Of love and loss in the night.

In the quiet, the soul can see,
Reflections of what's meant to be.
With every shadow, serenity grows,
As the gentle night unfolds and glows.

Let the moments linger near,
Embracing all we hold dear.
In the shadows, we find our song,
A melody where we belong.

Layers of Life's Tapestry

Threads of gold and hues of grey,
We weave the stories day by day.
With each stitch, a memory sewn,
In the fabric, our lives are known.

Soft whispers bound in every seam,
Echoes of laughter, love, and dream.
Pain and joy, they intertwine,
Creating patterns, yours and mine.

The tapestry flows, a river wide,
Holding treasures we can't hide.
Every wrinkle, and every crease,
Symbols of struggle, heart, and peace.

Colors fade, yet they remain,
Each layer speaks of joy and pain.
Bound together, we walk the line,
In life's tapestry, we intertwine.

So let us cherish every shade,
In this masterpiece we have made.
For every layer tells a tale,
In life's grand weave, we shall not pale.

Canvas of Existence

On life's canvas, bold and wide,
We paint our hopes, with love our guide.
Every stroke, a heartbeat shared,
In every shade, our souls are bared.

From shadows deep to gleaming light,
Our spirits soar, taking flight.
With dreams unbound, the brush does glide,
Creating worlds where we reside.

The canvas breathes with every tear,
As colors mingle, drawing near.
In the chaos, we find our way,
Turning night into a brighter day.

Every art piece tells the tale,
Of love, of loss, or dreams that sailed.
In vibrant hues, our lives converse,
On this vast canvas, we immerse.

So let us paint with hearts afire,
Crafting visions that inspire.
In this canvas of existence true,
We find ourselves, and start anew.

Echoes of the Heartbeat

In the silence, whispers dwell,
A rhythm soft, a silent spell.
Each pulse a tale, a love once known,
In shadows deep, its truth is sown.

Through the night, memories glide,
An endless dance, a gentle tide.
Hearts entwined in a warm embrace,
Resounding echoes our sacred space.

Time weaves on, a thread so fine,
Marking moments, a lifeline's sign.
In every beat, a story thrives,
With echoes strong, our spirit dives.

Each heartbeat sings of days long past,
In every truth, forever cast.
From joy to pain, each note they chart,
In silent halls, resides the heart.

Listen close, to whispers near,
Let love's song be crystal clear.
For in the heartbeat lies the key,
Unlocking dreams in harmony.

Whirls of the Universe

Stars collide in a cosmic dance,
Galaxies sway in a timeless trance.
Stardust twirls on celestial breeze,
Whispers of light through the ancient trees.

Planets spin in a spiral sea,
Bound by gravity, wild and free.
In every orbit, a secret dwells,
Of life beyond, where magic swells.

Nebulas bloom in colors bright,
Crafting dreams in the velvet night.
In distant realms, where echoes play,
Whirls of wonder lead the way.

Comets blaze with a fiery tail,
Charting paths in a starlit trail.
The universe sings a timeless song,
In its vast arms, we all belong.

So gaze above at the endless sky,
Feel the whirls as they lift us high.
In unity, we find our place,
In the cosmos' grand, embracing space.

The Canvas of Tomorrow

Brushstrokes bright on a canvas wide,
Dreams unfold as colors collide.
In hues of hope, visions ignite,
Crafting a path through the quiet night.

Every splash tells a story grand,
Whispers of futures, by heart and hand.
Creativity blooms where shadows lie,
Painting tomorrow as we reach for the sky.

With every stroke, possibilities rise,
A tapestry woven, a brilliant guise.
In the palette of life, shades intertwine,
We blend our truths, make visions align.

Through trials faced, as we voyage near,
Artistry blossoms from every fear.
In the canvas bright, where dreams convene,
We chart the unknown, wild and serene.

So paint your heart, let the colors flow,
For tomorrow's light will always glow.
In the artwork of life, brave and bold,
Our stories gleam in strokes of gold.

Illumination in Shadows

In twilight's grasp, shadows convene,
A world disguised, yet still unseen.
Flickers of light through the darkness play,
Guiding lost souls along their way.

Each shadow whispers secrets deep,
In silent corners, where spirits creep.
Illuminated dreams dance on the brink,
With every heartbeat, we stop and think.

Moonlight drapes its silver veil,
Lending strength to the fragile trail.
In quiet moments, we find our grace,
Embracing the light in a hidden place.

Stars ignite in the velvety night,
Filling the void with their shimmering light.
Illumination sparks a vibrant path,
Transforming shadows with love's warm wrath.

So fear not the dark; let your heart see,
That light's presence is always free.
In the shadows, love's flame will glow,
Illumination's dance forever flows.

Labyrinth of Inspiration

In the maze of thoughts we wander,
Twisting paths that pull and ponder.
Every turn a fresh new view,
Whispers of dreams call us through.

Ink-stained fingers dance and play,
Sketching visions on display.
Hopes and fears entwined so tight,
In the depths, we find our light.

Each corner holds a story bright,
Shadows fade to morning light.
Follow trails of heart's desire,
Ignite the soul, set it on fire.

Listen close, the echoes gleam,
In this labyrinth, we dare to dream.
With every step, the journey grows,
Inspiration's river slowly flows.

Let the heart's compass guide the way,
Through the night to find the day.
In this maze, we come alive,
Inspiration's breath helps us thrive.

Mithril Tapestry

Threads of silver softly gleam,
Weaving tales that rise and dream.
Each strand a whisper, silk and bold,
A tapestry of life unfolds.

Colors blend in vibrant hue,
Stories ancient, ever new.
Stitches placed with tender care,
Woven love hangs in the air.

Patterns dance, a gentle sway,
Echoes from the yesterday.
Fingers tracing every line,
A legacy in each design.

Mithril gleams under starlit skies,
Crafted where the heart complies.
In this art, our souls unite,
Embodied dreams in purest light.

As we weave, our spirits rise,
In this quilt, our love never lies.
With every thread, we boldly chart,
A timeless bond, a work of heart.

Renewal in Color

When spring arrives with blooms so bright,
Nature's brush ignites delight.
Violets whisper, daisies sing,
Renewal flows on vibrant wings.

Colors splash against the gray,
Painting hope in bold array.
Life awakens, gently stirs,
In every petal, love occurs.

From barren branches, leaves emerge,
In this cycle, dreams converge.
Through rainbows cast and skies so blue,
Nature whispers, start anew.

The sunbeams kiss the earth's embrace,
Every moment, a sacred space.
With every dawn, a chance to rise,
In vibrant hues, we touch the skies.

In this season, hearts ignite,
Color spills, a pure delight.
Renewal sings in life's sweet song,
In every shade, we all belong.

The Light and the Shade

In the dance of light and dark,
Whispers echo, leaving a mark.
Shadows play where secrets hide,
In the twilight, dreams abide.

Sunrise paints the world anew,
Gentle hues in every view.
Moonlight casts its silver glow,
In the stillness, time moves slow.

Every shadow tells a tale,
Silent stories that unveil.
Within the dark, a spark ignites,
Hope emerges in the nights.

Balance found in every heart,
Light and shade, they never part.
Through the contrast, we find grace,
In life's journey, we embrace.

Together they weave a song,
In their embrace, we all belong.
In light and shade, we learn to see,
The beauty in our duality.

Colors of Connection

In crimson hues, we find our start,
Each shade a beat within the heart.
From blue to gold, our spirits soar,
In every color, love's sweet lore.

Emerald dreams in twilight's grace,
A tapestry of time and space.
The art we make, together bright,
Illuminating endless night.

With every stroke, our stories blend,
A canvas bright, where hearts transcend.
Together in this vibrant sea,
We paint the bond of you and me.

As colors dance in perfect rhyme,
We forge connections, deep as time.
With each embrace, the spectrum swells,
In hues of joy, our spirit dwells.

So let us weave our dreams in light,
Transforming darkness into bright.
In every shade, our voices ring,
In this connection, love takes wing.

Paths in the Palette

Upon the canvas, life unfolds,
In brushstrokes bold, our journey told.
The paths we take, each hue a guide,
In vibrant tones where dreams reside.

With every footprint, colors blend,
Invisible ties that never end.
From hues of red to calming blue,
Each step we take, a chance to view.

The whispers of the palette call,
Inviting us to rise, not fall.
In every shade, a story we trace,
Navigating through time and space.

Emerging shades of green and gold,
In every moment, courage bold.
Paths intertwine, our lives align,
In artistry, our hearts combine.

Together dancing through the night,
Hand in hand, we chase the light.
In paths of color, we find our way,
Creating beauty day by day.

The Symphony of Creation

In every note, a heartbeat sings,
Resonating with the joy it brings.
The symphony of life unfolds,
In melodies, our tale retold.

From silence, sound begins to rise,
A dance of rhythm beneath the skies.
With strings and winds, we craft our fate,
An opus bright, we cultivate.

Harmony in every voice,
In unity, we find our choice.
Through crescendos, whispers fly,
In creation's breath, we learn to fly.

A sonnet spun in colors bold,
In every verse, a dream retold.
Together crafting every line,
In this grand score, our souls entwine.

With every chord, our spirits swell,
In the symphony, we know so well.
Each note a color, vibrant, true,
Together, we compose anew.

Vivid Echoes of Life

In shadows cast by fading light,
Vivid echoes take their flight.
Through whispers soft, we hear the past,
In each embrace, the die is cast.

Colors clash in vibrant scenes,
Life's tapestry, the thread it weaves.
From gentle murmur to thunder's call,
Each echo beckons, inviting all.

We paint our dreams in shades so bright,
With every heartbeat, pure delight.
In laughter shared, in tears we find,
The vivid echoes of our mind.

Fractals dancing, time stands still,
In every moment, a potent thrill.
Through all we face, we rise and dive,
In vivid colors, we come alive.

So let us cherish every sound,
In echoes bright, our hopes abound.
In life's great canvas, we discover,
Each vibrant tone, a gift from cover.

Stories Woven in Time

In the twilight of yesteryears,
Echoes of laughter softly chime.
Threads of memory, woven tight,
Unravel tales that dance in light.

Each whisper carries a soft embrace,
A tapestry of dreams we chase.
With every heartbeat and sigh,
We etch our stories in the sky.

The pages turn, the ink will dry,
But histories linger, they never die.
In shadows cast by fading sun,
The journey's end is just begun.

From elders' eyes to youthful fire,
We seek the spark that lifts us higher.
In every glance, a chapter shared,
The legacy of love declared.

So gather close, my dear old friend,
With every tale, we start to mend.
These woven whispers, soft and kind,
Are stories that forever bind.

Curves of Connection

In shadows deep, our voices blend,
The dance of souls, where paths extend.
A silent vow, in whispers found,
Together strong, we stand our ground.

With gentle grace, the moments weave,
A tapestry of love, believe.
In every glance, a spark ignites,
Uniting hearts on starry nights.

Through winding trails, our steps may roam,
In every heartbeat, we feel at home.
Each curve a story, each bend a song,
In this connection, we all belong.

The Color of Now

In the canvas of the present hour,
Brushstrokes bathe in vibrant power.
Each moment glimmers, bold and bright,
A kaleidoscope of pure delight.

The sunbeam dances on petals fair,
While whispers of wind play with our hair.
The laughter of children, sweet and clear,
Paints joy in hues that draw us near.

With every heartbeat, colors shift,
A fleeting glance, a timely gift.
The sky's embrace, a canvas vast,
Where shadows linger, but never last.

In every sigh, a shade we find,
Moments captured, intertwined.
The rhythm of life, a vibrant glow,
In the pulse of now, let love flow.

So let us savor this radiant view,
With open hearts, we start anew.
For in the color of each breath,
Lies the beauty of life and death.

Muse of the Mundane

In the quiet corners of the day,
Life unfolds in a delicate way.
The mundane whispers soft and low,
Yet hides the magic we often forgo.

A cup of tea, the warmth it brings,
The rustle of leaves, the joy it sings.
In simple tasks, a beauty found,
In the rhythm of life, we are bound.

With every breath, we craft a line,
In mundane moments, the stars align.
So hold the fleeting seconds dear,
Each heartbeat whispers, "I am here."

The dance of chores, a subtle art,
Transforms the ordinary into heart.
In laundry's fold, a story spins,
In the cycle of life, our laughter begins.

So let's embrace the day-to-day,
With open hands, let worries sway.
In the muse of the mundane, we find,
A world abundant and intertwined.

Tones of Tranquility

Amidst the leaves, soft whispers sigh,
A melody that floats on high.
The world slows down, a gentle pause,
Nature's heartbeat, without a cause.

Blue skies embrace the golden sun,
In calm embrace, all races run.
The river hums a soothing tune,
Reflecting peace beneath the moon.

In silent moments, we find our place,
The quietude, a warm embrace.
With every breath, serenity flows,
In the tones of tranquility, love grows.

Whirlwind of the Creative Spirit

In the eye of a storm, ideas swirl,
A tempest of thought, a vibrant twirl.
The canvas beckons, wild and free,
Where dreams take flight, unbound esprit.

Across the sky, colors collide,
As inspiration's waves begin to ride.
With every stroke, a world awakes,
Enchanted journeys our spirit makes.

The nightingale's song, a sweet refrain,
Ignites the fire, and passion's gain.
In chaos, clarity may emerge,
In every surge, our souls converge.

Let thoughts be rivers, flowing wide,
With every twist, let visions glide.
In the whirlwind's dance, we rise and spin,
Creativity's pulse resonating within.

So breathe in deeply, let the wind play,
With eyes alight, we shape our way.
In the whirlwind of spirit, we create,
A universe vast, a future innate.

Flourishing in Chaos

In storms of life, we bend and sway,
Roots dig deep, come what may.
Amidst the turmoil, flowers bloom,
Finding light in darkest gloom.

With vibrant colors, hearts collide,
In chaos, we learn to abide.
Resilience rises, fierce and bold,
A story of strength, waiting to unfold.

Through tangled paths, we find our way,
In every challenge, we choose to stay.
Flourishing fiercely, we take our stand,
Together, we thrive, hand in hand.

The Poetry of Brush and Canvas

In colors bright, the artist dreams,
With every stroke, the canvas gleams.
A whisper soft, the brush does dance,
Creating worlds in a silent trance.

Each hue a tale, each line a song,
Where visions bloom, and hearts belong.
The palette sings in vibrant swirls,
As beauty flows, through life it twirls.

In every shade, a story waits,
Of hopes and fears, of love and fates.
With every layer, depth reveals,
The soul of art, the heart it steals.

Beneath the gaze, the colors blend,
An endless journey with no end.
The brush, it knows, the truth untold,
In every masterpiece, dreams unfold.

A silent bond, the artist's touch,
In every piece, a part of us.
The poetry lies in what we see,
In brush and canvas, we are free.

Melodies of the Artisan's Path

A craftsman's hands, so deft and sure,
In every cut, a sound so pure.
With wood and stone, the echoes soar,
Melodies formed, forever more.

The hammer strikes, a rhythmic beat,
In chisels sharp, the art's complete.
With every press, the spirit sings,
Of timeless joy and simple things.

From thread to fabric, stitches weave,
A tapestry of dreams conceived.
In colors bright, the patterns dance,
Life's melodies in every chance.

Crafting moments in the twilight,
An artisan's heart, a guiding light.
In shadows cast, the stories flow,
Of passion deep, a vibrant glow.

To hands that mold, and hearts that care,
In every piece, a love laid bare.
The path we walk, the dreams we chase,
Melodies of time, a warm embrace.

Chronicles of Creativity

A blank page waits, a world untold,
In scribbles soft, the mind unfolds.
With ink and thought, the story grows,
In every line, the heart bestows.

From dreams at night to dawn's first light,
Imagination takes its flight.
With every word, new realms ignite,
In chronicles of pure delight.

The artist's pen, a wand of grace,
In letters formed, new lives embrace.
With voices bold, and whispers shy,
The tales we weave will never die.

Through trials faced, and triumphs won,
Each chapter starts, a new begun.
In creativity, we find our way,
A journey rich, come what may.

So let the ink flow, let dreams ignite,
In chronicles of every light.
We pen our fate, with hearts so free,
In words and art, we find our glee.

Harmonies in Hues

A symphony of colors bright,
In every shade, a pure delight.
With strokes of blue and splashes red,
Harmonies in hues are bred.

Each canvas sings a heart's refrain,
In joyous greens and vibrant grain.
The colors blend, creating peace,
In every stroke, a sweet release.

A dance of tones, a fleeting glance,
In art's embrace, we take a chance.
With each new blend, our spirits sway,
Harmonious hues, come what may.

In sunlight's glow, the colors play,
As shadows shift, and brightens day.
A palette rich with stories told,
In every hue, a treasure holds.

So let us paint this world anew,
With passion's fire and dreams so true.
In harmonies of bright delight,
In hues we bask, and hearts take flight.

The Gallery of Being

In every heartbeat, a canvas bright,
Brushstrokes of laughter, shadows of night.
Each moment captured, a piece of time,
In the gallery of being, we all climb.

Frame by frame, our stories unfold,
Whispers of dreams, both timid and bold.
A collection of memories, laughter and tears,
Each portrait reflecting our hopes and fears.

With colors colliding, the past and now,
We stand in awe, take a humble bow.
In every glance, the art becomes clear,
The gallery of being, forever near.

The Heart's Composition

In chambers deep where feelings dwell,
A symphony of shadows swell.
Notes of joy, a hint of pain,
Crafting love in soft refrain.

Rhythms beat, a steady sound,
In every heartbeat, grace is found.
Each silence speaks, a hidden tune,
Under the watchful gaze of moon.

The heart, a canvas filled with light,
Brush strokes vivid, day and night.
With every pulse, the story flows,
In tender whispers, secrets grows.

Harmony of spirit, pure and bright,
Chasing dreams, igniting the night.
Each emotion, a brush of fate,
In the gallery of love, we wait.

Together we paint, our lives entwined,
With strokes of truth that won't unwind.
In this art of souls, our decree,
A masterpiece of you and me.

Strokes of Whispering Hues

Colors dance on canvas wide,
Every stroke a feeling inside.
Whispers of blue, echoes of red,
In shades of passion, hearts are fed.

Gentle swirls of emerald grace,
Bringing life to a static space.
Gold and silver, the light they weave,
Painting stories we can't believe.

In the silence, colors speak,
A language bold, though soft and meek.
Brushes gliding, a rhythmic flight,
Crafting visions in soft twilight.

Contours merge, embracing tight,
Filling the canvas with pure delight.
Vivid dreams take shape and soar,
Beyond the ether, to distant shore.

With every hue, a world unfolds,
In every heartbeat, a tale retold.
Colors whisper in twilight's glow,
Inviting souls to come and flow.

Crafting the Unseen

In shadows deep where dreams reside,
We sculpt the visions cast aside.
With quiet hands, we mold the air,
Creating realms that dare to share.

The unsaid speaks in softest tones,
In silence, echoes of our bones.
Forming shapes that bend the light,
Crafting beauty from darkest night.

Imaginations take their flight,
Dancing in the pale moonlight.
With every breath, a world is spun,
In the tapestry of all that's begun.

We weave the fabric of our minds,
In every thread, the heart unwinds.
From whispers soft, the unseen gleams,
Painting shadows with vivid dreams.

The canvas whispers, secrets told,
Hand in hand, we break the mold.
In the art of crafting what's concealed,
Life's hidden treasures are revealed.

The Burst of Creativity

In quiet moments, sparks ignite,
Imagination takes to flight.
Ideas bloom like flowers fair,
In the garden of the mind, they dare.

Colors burst, a vivid stream,
Rivers of thought, a flowing dream.
Each concept weaves a brand new thread,
Creating paths where none have tread.

From chaos springs the purest form,
In tempest's eye, a gentle storm.
With brush and tongue, we shape the unknown,
Crafting worlds from seeds we've sown.

Let passion roar, let spirits rise,
In bursts of joy, we claim the skies.
Every heartbeat, a brand new start,
In this explosion of the heart.

Together we spark the flame,
Unleashing art, that has no name.
The burst of creativity flies,
In wild abandon, we touch the skies.

The Choreography of Life

In the dance of day and night,
We twist and turn in fading light.
Each step a choice, each breath a song,
Together we find where we belong.

With partners lost and friendships found,
We waltz amid the joyous sound.
Life's rhythm beats in subtle ways,
Guiding us through the fleeting days.

In shadows deep, the spotlight glows,
We move to where the heartache goes.
Each stumble wears our stories well,
In every slip, a truth to tell.

As seasons change, the music shifts,
We learn to wade through life's great rifts.
Every note both sharp and sweet,
A harmony we all must meet.

A final bow, the curtain falls,
In whispered dreams, our spirit calls.
The choreography of our days,
In every step, love's gentle gaze.

The Brush of Transformation

With every stroke, we redefine,
A canvas blank, a heart divine.
Colors blend in vibrant hue,
Each layer tells of what rings true.

The brush dances through trials and grace,
Crafting visions time can't erase.
Dreams unfold with every swipe,
Awakening the soul's rich type.

In shades of doubt, in strokes of hope,
We paint our paths, we learn to cope.
Each hue a tale, each line a mark,
Illuminating light in dark.

As seasons change, the palette grows,
Against the canvas, life bestows.
With gentle hands, we craft anew,
Transforming all we thought we knew.

A masterpiece in progress stands,
A testament to life's commands.
With every brush, a vision born,
In the quiet, we are reborn.

A Symphony in Silence

Between the notes, a story flows,
In whispered dreams, the silence grows.
Unspoken words fill the empty air,
In quietude, we learn to care.

The hush of night, the break of dawn,
Each moment sings, though words seem gone.
The heartbeats merge in softest sound,
In stillness, life's rich echoes found.

Soft shadows dance, no need for voice,
In silent depths, our souls rejoice.
The symphony of what's unwritten,
In pauses, love's true path is smitten.

In solitude, the world expands,
The unseen beauty in quiet lands.
A melody without a strain,
A gentle touch, like softest rain.

Let silence wrap us, hold us tight,
In every breath, there's pure delight.
Together in this wordless song,
We find the peace where we belong.

Vignettes of the Soul

In fleeting glimpses, stories flow,
Each moment captured, seeds we sow.
A smile shared, a tear bestowed,
In vignettes, life's true colors glowed.

Through subtle echoes, whispers soft,
The tapestry we weave aloft.
Each thread a tale, each knot a chance,
To understand our soul's own dance.

In laughter bright and sorrow's ache,
The richness of our truths we make.
Fragments of joy, a hint of pain,
In every vignette, love will reign.

As moments pass, the heart's embrace,
In simple gestures, find our place.
A flicker, a flash, a lasting glow,
In captured time, our spirits grow.

These vignettes form a wondrous whole,
Each chapter enhances our soul.
With every breath, our stories blend,
In life's great journey, hearts ascend.

Moments Captured in Color

Brush strokes dance on canvas bright,
Vivid hues embrace the light.
Memories linger, softly they blend,
In every shade, a story penned.

Whispers of joy, traces of sorrow,
Captured today, a promise of tomorrow.
Each splash tells secrets, the heart's refrain,
In colors of passion, in colors of pain.

Moments frozen, time stands still,
In every detail, a voice to fill.
Framed in a glance, emotions unfold,
In a palette of life, memories told.

Nature's beauty, a symphony bright,
In the morning dew, in the stars at night.
Every corner, a vibrant scene,
In the art of living, we find the serene.

Each canvas speaks, a language new,
Of laughter, of love, in every hue.
Moments captured, forever they stay,
In the gallery of life, they softly play.

The Essence of Creativity

Ideas bloom like flowers in spring,
In the mind's garden, thoughts take wing.
A spark ignites, the canvas awaits,
Imagination dances, it creates.

Each stroke, a heartbeat, a life anew,
Crafted from vision, bold and true.
Where dreams collide and visions merge,
In the realm of art, the soul will surge.

The whispers of muses, guiding hands,
Breaking like waves on distant sands.
Chaos and order, a delicate thread,
In the tapestry woven, emotions are fed.

Colors collide, a cacophony bright,
In shadows that flicker in soft twilight.
From silence emerges a voice profound,
In the essence of creativity, magic is found.

With every creation, they stake their claim,
In the endless pursuit of a beautiful name.
Imagination's power, wild and free,
In the heart of the artist, lies eternity.

Crafting Tomorrow's Dreams

Amidst the whispers of quiet night,
Dreams take shape, bathed in light.
Sketches of hope on paper reside,
In the artist's heart, visions collide.

Threads of tomorrow are woven today,
In imagined worlds where we all play.
With every detail, a castle of dreams,
Where nothing is ever as simple as seems.

Painting the future with vibrant hues,
In the art of creation, we choose.
From seeds of thought, great wonders grow,
In the fields of possibility, we sow.

Bridges of talents, connect and align,
In the symphony written, all hearts combine.
In the realm of the future, we build and we strive,
Crafting a tapestry where dreams come alive.

With every heartbeat, we shape our fate,
In the canvas of time, we iterate.
Tomorrow awaits in colors so bright,
In the dreams we weave, we find our light.

The Soul's Canvas

In the depths of silence, the soul speaks loud,
On its canvas, dreams are proud.
Each stroke, a reflection, deep and real,
In hues of passion, the heart will feel.

Layers of emotions, a story unfolds,
In every corner, a mystery holds.
With wisdom of ages, the brush conveys,
The essence of life in myriad ways.

Moments linger, like shadows at dusk,
Crafting the light with a vibrant musk.
In the soul's embrace, we find the true sight,
The canvas of being, a dance in the light.

Threads of existence, a tapestry grand,
stitched by the heart, with a gentle hand.
In shades of laughter and tones of pain,
The soul's canvas holds everything sane.

In the gallery of life, color meets grace,
An ever-evolving, a timeless embrace.
With every heartbeat, we paint our way,
On the soul's canvas, forever we'll stay.

Serenity in Strokes

In twilight's hush, the canvas glows,
Whispers of peace in every pose.
Gentle hues, a soft embrace,
Finding calm in this quiet space.

Each stroke a sigh, a moment drawn,
As day departs and dreams are spawned.
Let colors blend, let shadows sigh,
In art we trust, our spirits fly.

The brush caresses, the heart beats slow,
Emotions dance, a tender flow.
With every layer, a story told,
In every stroke, a memory gold.

Serenity formed in vibrant threads,
An artist's heart, where stillness spreads.
Through hues of blue and gold so bright,
We weave tranquility into the night.

In every corner, a world unveiled,
In every detail, the soul curtailed.
Find refuge here, a place to dream,
In strokes of peace, let your heart beam.

The Rhythm of Life

In morning light, new hopes arise,
With beating hearts and open skies.
Life's melody, the sweetest tune,
With every dawn, a chance to bloom.

Moments dance, like shadows play,
The rhythm guides us through the day.
With laughter shared and tearful sighs,
We weave our tales beneath wide skies.

In hurried steps or gentle pace,
Life finds its groove, a sacred space.
With every heartbeat, a story's spun,
In the rhythm of life, we are one.

From whispered dreams to bold pursuits,
Life's symphony in roots and shoots.
In every pulse, a chance to thrive,
In every breath, the will to strive.

So dance along this vibrant road,
Embrace the rhythm, lighten your load.
For in this journey, we all belong,
In the rhythm of life, we are strong.

Brushstrokes and Breaths

With every brushstroke, a heartbeat felt,
In colors mixed, emotions melt.
The canvas breathes, a living scene,
Where dreams are stitched, serene, unseen.

Each line a journey, a path to seek,
Whispers of truth in what we speak.
The artist's eye, a window wide,
In brushstrokes bold, our souls confide.

In tranquil moments, we capture light,
In every shade, the day turns bright.
Through strokes of passion, hearts ignite,
As colors blend, we find our sight.

We breathe the art, we live the lines,
In every splash, a spark defines.
Together woven, a story spun,
In brushstrokes and breaths, we are one.

Let canvas cradle our deepest thought,
In vibrant strokes, the battles fought.
A dance of hues, a life expressed,
In brushstrokes and breaths, we are blessed.

Threads of Inspiration

In woven dreams, the threads align,
Each twist and turn, a tale divine.
With gentle hands, we craft our fate,
In strands of hope, we elevate.

The fabric speaks in colors bright,
With every stitch, we weave the light.
In hearts entwined, in moments shared,
Through threads of love, we show we cared.

In patterns bold, in whispers soft,
We celebrate what lifts us aloft.
Through tangled knots and fraying seams,
We navigate the maze of dreams.

In every loop, a promise we make,
With every knot, a bond we stake.
Together spinning, together bound,
In threads of inspiration, hope is found.

So gather close, let stories flow,
In fabric's embrace, let spirits grow.
For in our threads, we find our song,
In threads of inspiration, we belong.

The Palette of Days

Sunrise spills gold on the canvas wide,
Birds trace the sky, where shadows hide.
Colors emerge from the night's embrace,
Each moment captured, a fleeting grace.

Brush strokes dance in the morning glow,
Whispers of time in each soft flow.
In every hue, a story is spun,
Life's vivid tale has just begun.

Soft lilacs bloom in the breeze so light,
Crimson's blush paints the heart so bright.
Nature's laughter in a vibrant hue,
Each shade a memory, each tone is true.

Golden hours weave into twilight's thread,
With every color, a life we've led.
A masterpiece formed from trials and dreams,
In the palette of days, hope gently gleams.

As shadows stretch and the sun sinks low,
The canvas of dusk begins to glow.
Each stroke a heartbeat, a moment to share,
In the palette of days, we linger there.

Whispers of the Brush

The brush whispers tales on a canvas white,
With every stroke, it ignites the night.
A dance of colors in soft embrace,
Emotions come alive, time moves with grace.

Echoes of laughter in splashes of blue,
A testament to dreams that once flew.
Each line a memory, each dot a dream,
From the whispers of the brush, visions redeem.

With every swirl, the heart reveals,
Hidden truths that the soul conceals.
A landscape of thoughts in vibrant hue,
The art of feeling, the brave and the true.

Brushes tremble as stories unfold,
In the dance of creation, the brave and the bold.
Life's tender moments in textures unknown,
In whispers of the brush, we find our home.

Vibrant echoes of sunsets collide,
Each shadow and light, a journey inside.
With each stroke new, we find and we lose,
In whispers of the brush, we choose to muse.

Threads of Creation

Golden threads weave through the heart of night,
Knots of brilliance in the soft twilight.
Weaving stories through colors and forms,
In threads of creation, the spirit warms.

Every stitch sings of dreams yet to brew,
A fabric of thoughts, in the quiet few.
Textures collide, bringing life to the still,
Crafting a tale with an artist's will.

From whispers of laughter to sighs of the old,
Each thread a story, a moment retold.
In the tapestry's weave, we find what is true,
Threads of creation, connecting me to you.

With colors that bleed, merge, and entwine,
The fabric of time, in patterns divine.
Seasons of thought in vibrant display,
Threads of creation guide the way.

In each woven strand, emotions ignite,
A dance of the heart in warm moonlight.
Together we stitch, together we dream,
In threads of creation, life flows like a stream.

Echoes in Color

In the silence, echoes softly play,
Colors emerge, come what may.
Hues that whisper of moments gone,
In the tapestry of time, they carry on.

Like raindrops falling on a parched ground,
In echoes of color, new life is found.
Purples and greens twirl in a dance,
Creating a symphony, a fleeting chance.

Echoes of joy in brilliant reds,
In the warmth of the night where the dreamer treads.
Every shade speaks of love and despair,
In whispers of color, we breathe in the air.

As twilight drapes its silken veil,
Echoes in color tell a tale.
Shadows of memories in soft array,
In the language of art, we find our way.

So let us dance in the colors bright,
In echoes of life, find our delight.
For in every stroke, our spirits will soar,
In echoes in color, forever explore.

Whispers of a Dreaming Heart

In the stillness of the night,
Dreams take flight in softest light.
Whispers echo, gentle and clear,
Filling the silence, drawing near.

Stars twinkle with secrets untold,
Each one a story, daring and bold.
The heart listens, feeling the sway,
Guided by hope, it dances away.

Moonlight drapes a silver hue,
Caressing thoughts, tender and true.
In shadows deep, inspiration gleams,
Painting the world with vibrant dreams.

A symphony of wishes arise,
Carried on whispers, lit by the skies.
Each heartbeat echoes the timeless quest,
To seek the magic, to feel the blessed.

When dawn breaks, the dreams will stay,
In every moment, come what may.
For in the heart, they dwell and breathe,
A tapestry woven, weaves and seethes.

Journey Through a Kaleidoscope

Splashes of color, vibrant and bright,
Shapes twist and turn, a wondrous sight.
Through shattered glass, visions unfold,
Stories emerge, both new and old.

A dance of patterns, endlessly swirls,
Secrets encased, as the world twirls.
Every glance reveals a new view,
In each moment, find something true.

Glimmers of joy in fragments appear,
Hope hidden softly, ever so near.
Step into realms where dreams collide,
Discover the beauty that lies inside.

A fleeting journey, yet timeless it seems,
In colors and shapes, the heart truly beams.
Embrace the chaos, let visions run wild,
For life's a canvas, forever beguiled.

With every turn, new paths reveal,
The wonder of life in each vivid reel.
Through the kaleidoscope, make your mark,
In swirling hues, ignite the spark.

Finding Beauty in the Unseen

In shadows deep, where silence lies,
Hidden wonders begin to rise.
A fragile bloom in cracks of stone,
Whispers of life, felt but not shown.

The gentle rustle of leaves at night,
Echoes of laughter, just out of sight.
In the fleeting glance, in glimmers fast,
Beauty resides, forever cast.

A spider's web, adorned with dew,
Reflects the dawn in morning's hue.
Moments of stillness, often obscured,
Hold the richness of hearts assured.

In every sigh, in every tear,
A tapestry woven, drawing near.
Finding the grace in what's left behind,
Beauty whispers softly, yet so kind.

Explore the quiet, the soft, the small,
In hidden places, hear nature's call.
For in the unseen, our souls take flight,
Embracing the magic of gentle light.

Footprints of the Imagination

On the sandy shores of thought's embrace,
Footprints linger, a tender trace.
Each step a story, each path a dream,
Flowing like rivers, a timeless stream.

Glimpses of worlds we've yet to explore,
Infinite realms behind each door.
In the echoes of laughter, joy takes form,
Creativity blooms, wild and warm.

Through forests deep and skies so vast,
Imagination flies, free and fast.
Every twist and turn holds a spark,
Guiding each heart through the dark.

With colors splashed upon the night,
Visions awaken, taking flight.
In the canvas of dreams, we paint our fate,
Footprints of wonder, never too late.

So wander freely, let your heart roam,
In the land of dreams, you're always home.
For in imagination's sweet delight,
We find our purpose, shining bright.

Luminescent Journeys

In the twilight's gentle glow,
Stars awaken, tales to show,
Paths illuminated, secrets gleam,
Wandering souls chase their dream.

Whispers of the night unfold,
Stories of the brave and bold,
Each step echoes through the air,
Guiding hearts with tender care.

Through the forest, shadows dance,
In the moonlight, take a chance,
With every turn, a new delight,
Luminescent paths ignite.

Rivers glisten, mountains high,
Where the eagles dare to fly,
Nature's palette, vibrant, free,
Painting dreams for all to see.

As we journey, hand in hand,
In this life, we make our stand,
Together facing every night,
Chasing futures, pure and bright.

The Craft of Living

In the silence of the morn,
Dreams awaken, hopes are born,
With each breath, a canvas wide,
Colors blend as worlds collide.

Moments fleeting, shadows cast,
Crafting memories that will last,
Weaving joy with threads of pain,
In life's fabric, all remain.

Hands that nurture, hearts that feel,
In this journey, wounds can heal,
An artist's touch in every fight,
The craft of living brings the light.

Through the chaos, finding peace,
In the storm, we find release,
With every laugh, with every tear,
Life's true beauty stays so near.

So let us dance through joy and strife,
Creating art, this precious life,
In every heartbeat, every sigh,
The craft of living will not die.

Brush with Destiny

With a stroke, the canvas waits,
Life unfolds, we shape our fates,
In the silence, visions bloom,
Brush with destiny, break the gloom.

Colors clash and merge as one,
In the shadows, battles won,
Each decision, a sacred path,
Crafting futures, light the math.

Whispers echo, choices call,
Rise or stumble, we must fall,
Yet with each descent we find,
Strength resides within the mind.

Time will paint with shades of grace,
Moments fleeting, we embrace,
Guided by that inner spark,
Navigating through the dark.

So let us wield our brush with care,
Crafting stories, dreams to share,
For in the art of what we seek,
Lives a promise, pure and meek.

A Palette of Experiences

On a canvas, life's array,
Vivid colors on display,
Every hue a tale to tell,
A palette rich, we weave our spell.

Crimson joys and sapphire tears,
Golden hopes that conquer fears,
Painting passion, strokes of love,
Underneath the skies above.

Every brushstroke, laughter sings,
Memories dance on vibrant wings,
In the night, where shadows meet,
Life's great art, both bittersweet.

With every hue, we learn anew,
The beauty in the trials too,
Canvas stretched, and hearts laid bare,
In every corner, we find care.

A masterpiece of shared embrace,
We find ourselves in time and space,
Through every shade, we journey on,
A palette rich, life's colors drawn.

Flourishes of the Soul

In quiet corners, whispers grow,
The heart's soft melody, a gentle flow.
Each laugh and tear, a vibrant hue,
Moments captured, pure and true.

Wings of hope in a stormy night,
Carrying dreams on fragile flight.
Boundless grace, in each embrace,
A tapestry woven, time can't erase.

In gardens where the wildflowers bloom,
Life's fragrance dances, dispelling gloom.
Roots of kindness deep in the ground,
In every soul, love's echoes resound.

The sun paints skies with crimson and gold,
Stories of courage begin to unfold.
Each heartbeat a rhythm, strong and bold,
Life's shared journey, beautifully told.

So let us wander, hand in hand,
Through fields of wonder, where dreams expand.
For in the flourishes, we find our way,
A symphony of souls, come what may.

Fragments of a Dream

In twilight's glow, dreams take flight,
Whispers of magic in the night.
Stars weave tales in the velvet sky,
Where hopes and wishes softly lie.

A dance with shadows, fleeting and bright,
Moments captured in ethereal light.
Time slips away like grains of sand,
Each fragment cherished, carefully planned.

Mirror reflections, a world anew,
Every vision held close and true.
Colors of yearning, painted in sighs,
Glances exchanged under cosmic skies.

With eyes wide open, we chase the dawn,
Finding our way as the night is drawn.
Every heartbeat a note in the song,
Fragments of dreams where we belong.

In the quiet moments between the beats,
Life's hidden treasures our heartache greets.
From dusk to dawn, a gentle embrace,
In fragments of dreams, we find our place.

Delicate Imprints

With every step, a story unfolds,
Delicate imprints, soft yet bold.
The earth remembers each gentle touch,
A quiet legacy, meaning so much.

In the whispers of leaves underfoot,
Nature's canvas where we are rooted.
Each petal's fall, a moment in time,
Every heartbeat a silent rhyme.

Glances exchanged in fleeting hours,
Moments gathered like springtime flowers.
Weaving memories in sun and shade,
In delicate imprints, love won't fade.

With every sunset that paints the sky,
A reminder that we, too, can fly.
In shadows cast, light will always shine,
Each imprint cherished, forever divine.

Through seasons of change, we will grow,
Leaving imprints, like footprints in snow.
In the dance of life, a rhythm we find,
Delicate imprints, forever aligned.

Reflections in Light

Beneath the surface, where dreams reside,
Reflections shimmer, our hopes as guides.
In pools of stillness, the soul takes flight,
Illuminating shadows with purest light.

Every moment a canvas, brushed with grace,
Capturing echoes, time's soft embrace.
The glow of laughter, the warmth of a smile,
In reflections in light, we reconcile.

Through the veil of twilight, soft secrets reveal,
Whispers of joy, in every appeal.
The dance of shadows, a playful event,
In the tapestry woven, our hearts are lent.

With every dawn, fresh dreams ignite,
Guiding our journey, a radiant sight.
Reflections of love shining brightly above,
Reminding us always of what we are loved.

So let the light guide us on this quest,
In moments of doubt, we are truly blessed.
For in every reflection, a story is spun,
In reflections of light, we are always one.

Harmony of the Heart

In whispers soft, the heart does sing,
Melodies of love on gentle wing.
Each beat a note, so sweetly played,
A symphony of dreams that never fade.

With every glance, a story we weave,
In quiet moments, we believe.
Together we dance through life's grand tune,
A harmony that blooms under the moon.

Through trials faced, our bond grows strong,
An endless echo, a cherished song.
In laughter shared and tears we part,
The timeless rhythm of the heart.

With every dawn, new hope appears,
The joy we find dispels our fears.
As day gives way to stars in sight,
Our hearts unite in love's pure light.

In tender moments, we take our stand,
Two souls entwined, hand in hand.
In this duet, we play our part,
A symphony, the harmony of the heart.

The Sculptor's Touch

With chisel firm, he carves the stone,
Each stroke a whisper, not alone.
Chiseling dreams from marble white,
He finds the form, brings it to light.

Every curve speaks of time and grace,
A story told on a timeless face.
In silent strength, the figure stands,
Crafted by skilled and gentle hands.

The dust settles, a gallery born,
Artistry flows since the day he sworn.
To breathe life into dreams anew,
In every piece, his vision grew.

Through trials faced with patience and care,
He shapes the world, a sculptor rare.
With each creation, a piece of soul,
In marble hearts, he makes them whole.

In shadows cast and light so clear,
He carves the visions we hold dear.
With every touch, a voice that speaks,
Transcending time, the art he seeks.

Symphony of Surroundings

The rustling leaves in a gentle breeze,
Nature's song, a tune that frees.
With every chirp, the world awakes,
Alive in harmony as day breaks.

The mountains rise like ancient kings,
Guarding secrets the forest brings.
Rivers flow in a graceful dance,
A symphony born of happenstance.

Clouds drift softly, a painter's brush,
Colors blending in the morning hush.
As shadows play on fields of gold,
Stories of old in silence told.

In every sound, a pulse we know,
The heartbeat of earth, steady and slow.
From dawn till dusk, the music flows,
A symphony that nature bestows.

With open hearts, we breathe it in,
The beauty wrapped in a world akin.
In every sigh and laughter bright,
We find our peace, wrapped in light.

Living in Strokes

A brush in hand, the canvas waits,
With colors bright, it celebrates.
Strokes of life in hues so bold,
Each twist and turn, a tale unfolds.

In splashes wild, emotions flow,
A universe in every glow.
With gentle strokes, the heart reveals,
The hidden truth that time conceals.

Shapes emerge from chaos so fine,
Stories captured in every line.
A dance of light, a play of shade,
In art, memories are displayed.

Textures whisper, colors sing,
A symphony that brush can bring.
In every piece, a part of me,
A glimpse of what it means to be.

In quiet moments, I lose my fears,
Each stroke a story through the years.
Living in strokes, forever free,
An artist's heart, in harmony.

Milton Keynes UK
Ingram Content Group UK Ltd.
UKHW022239280824
447491UK00010B/278